This
Book
Belongs
To _

Grolier Enterprises Inc.
SHERMAN TURNPIKE, DANBURY, CONNECTICUT 06816

Book Club Edition

The STORY Of DANIEL And The LIONS

An ALICE IN BIBLELAND Storybook®

Written by Alice Joyce Davidson
Illustrated by Victoria Marshall

Text copyright © 1000 by Alice Joyce Davidson
Art copyright © 1986 by The C.R. Gibson Company
Published by The C.R. Gibson Company
Norwalk, Connecticut 06856
Printed in the United States of America
All rights reserved
ISBN 0-8378-5079-7
D.L. TO: 157-1986

A little girl named Alice
Had some favorite things to do.
She liked to read of animals
And spend time at the zoo.

A Bible story Alice chose
To read and read again
Was about a man named Daniel
And some lions in a den.

One night as she was reading
Before she went to bed,
An airmail bird brought her a note
And this is what it said:

"Reading is the magic key
To take you where you want to be."

The Bible storybook she held
Became a giant screen.
Alice walked on through to Bibleland
And came upon this scene.

She saw a man named Daniel
Who'd been captured as a lad
And brought to far off Babylon
To serve the king they had.

Those people prayed to many gods,
But three times every day,
Daniel prayed to the One True God
And followed in His way.

A king named Darius ruled Babylon.
His kingdom was so large and grand
That he chose many leaders
To help him rule his land.

Of all the chosen leaders,
Daniel was so good and wise
That he became the favored one
In King Darius' eyes.

The others envied Daniel.
They were jealous as can be
And tried to find some failings
As they watched him carefully.

They found nothing wrong with Daniel,
But noticed that he prayed a lot,
So they put their heads together
And came up with this plot.

The leaders who were jealous
Went to Darius and said,
"Oh, mighty king, we've made a law!"
And this is how it read.

"For thirty days no one shall pray
Nor ask for anything
From any god or anyone
Except our mighty king."

"This law is for all leaders,
All women and all men.
Break this law and you will face
Fierce lions in their den."

So Darius then signed the law,
But Daniel still did pray
To the One True God who loved him
And heard his prayers each day.

The others spied on Daniel,
Then reported what they saw,
Saying, "Daniel should be punished,
For he dared to break your law."

Now, Darius loved Daniel
So he tried till night-time came
To find a way to change the law
To which he'd signed his name.

But the leaders then reminded him
That this law was for all men
So Daniel must be thrown at once
Into the lions' den.

King Darius told Daniel,
"Your God to whom you pray,
Surely He will save you
For you followed in His way."

Then Daniel went into the den
Where the hungry lions stayed.
A great big rock sealed off the den
And Daniel prayed and prayed.

The lions walked around him.
They showed their long, sharp claws,
But Daniel kept on praying
While they licked their hungry jaws.

All night the king was worried,
And when the morning came,
He hurried to the lions' den
And called out Daniel's name.

"Daniel, Daniel, speak to me.
Are you alive in there?
Did the God to whom you pray
Keep you in His care?"

Daniel answered, "Yes, my king,
Though I was full of fright,
God's angel closed the lions' jaws
And kept me safe all night!"

The king was glad for Daniel.
He took him out, and then
He gathered Daniel's enemies
And threw them in the den.

The king then made a brand new law
For everyone that day:
"Worship Daniel's One True God
And follow in His way."

The time had come for Alice
To leave that Bible scene.
She went back home by walking through
Her special giant screen.

Then Alice thought of Daniel
And how his faith stayed strong,
And how he trusted God above
When trouble came along.

Daniel followed God's commandment
To worship Him alone,
So even in the lions' den
God's loving care was shown.

When Alice said her prayers that night,
In her heart she knew
That God who cared for Daniel
Would always bless her, too.

For God's kingdom is forever.
He saves the great and small.
And best of all, as Alice knows,
God loves us one and all.